CRYPTO BASICS

A Beginner's Guide to Blockchain and Digital Currencies

JAMES T. FRALEY

Copyright © 2024 James T. Fraley

All rights reserved.

No piece of this book might be recreated or communicated in any structure or using any and all means, electronic or mechanical, including copying, recording, or by any data stockpiling and recovery framework, without composed consent from the writer, aside from the consideration of brief citations in a survey.

TABLE OF CONTENT

INTRODUCTION
- Why This Book Matters
- Who This Book is For
- How to Use This Book
- The Crypto Journey Begins

PART ONE UNDERSTANDING CRYPTOCURRENCIES
- CHAPTER ONE: WHAT IS CRYPTOCURRENCY?
- CHAPTER TWO: BLOCKCHAIN TECHNOLOGY 101
- CHAPTER THREE: KEY CRYPTOCURRENCIES
- CHAPTER FOUR: THE PURPOSE OF CRYPTOCURRENCIES
- PART ONE: WRAP-UP

PART TWO GETTING STARTED WITH CRYPTO
- CHAPTER FIVE: HOW TO BUY CRYPTOCURRENCY
- CHAPTER SIX: STORING CRYPTOCURRENCY SAFELY

- CHAPTER SEVEN: INVESTING IN CRYPTOCURRENCY
- PART TWO: WRAP-UP

PART THREE CRYPTO IN EVERYDAY LIFE

- CHAPTER EIGHT: REAL-WORLD APPLICATIONS
- CHAPTER NINE: REGULATIONS AND LEGAL ASPECTS
- CHAPTER TEN: THE FUTURE OF CRYPTOCURRENCY
- PART THREE WRAP-UP

CONCLUSION

APPENDICES

- Appendix A: Glossary of Key Terms
- Appendix B: FAQs on Cryptocurrencies
- Appendix C: Recommended Tools, Wallets, and Exchanges

CLOSING NOTE

INTRODUCTION

Welcome to *Crypto Basics*, your essential guide to understanding the revolutionary world of cryptocurrencies. Whether you're a complete beginner or someone with a basic understanding of digital assets, this book is designed to equip you with the knowledge and confidence to navigate this exciting and rapidly evolving space.

In the last decade, cryptocurrencies have transformed from a niche curiosity into a global phenomenon. Bitcoin, the first cryptocurrency, launched in 2009, sparked a movement that challenged traditional ideas about money, finance, and even technology itself. Today, cryptocurrencies are reshaping industries, powering innovation, and redefining how we think about ownership, value, and trust.

But what exactly are cryptocurrencies? How do they work? Why are they important? These are the questions this book will answer. We'll break down complex concepts into simple terms, provide real-world examples, and guide you through the practical steps of getting started with cryptocurrency.

WHY THIS BOOK MATTERS

The crypto world can feel overwhelming, filled with technical jargon, fluctuating markets, and a constant stream of new innovations. At its core, however, cryptocurrency represents something simple yet powerful: the ability to exchange value securely, transparently, and without unnecessary intermediaries.

Whether you're here out of curiosity, to explore investment opportunities, or to understand how crypto might impact your business or daily life, *Crypto Basics* will help you make informed decisions in this dynamic space.

WHO THIS BOOK IS FOR

This book is for anyone looking to demystify the world of cryptocurrency.

- **Beginners** who have heard about Bitcoin and Ethereum but don't know where to start.
- **Investors** interested in learning how cryptocurrencies fit into a broader portfolio.
- **Enthusiasts** curious about blockchain technology and its real-world applications.

No matter your background, we've structured this book to ensure you'll leave with a clear understanding of the fundamentals of crypto.

HOW TO USE THIS BOOK

The book is divided into three parts:

1. **Understanding Cryptocurrencies**: Laying the foundation with the key concepts, history, and technology behind crypto.
2. **Getting Started with Crypto**: Practical steps to buying, storing, and investing in cryptocurrencies.
3. **Crypto in Everyday Life**: Exploring how cryptocurrencies are being used today and what the future holds.

Each chapter builds upon the last, but feel free to jump to the sections that interest you most. We've included plenty of examples, tips, and resources along the way to support your learning journey.

THE CRYPTO JOURNEY BEGINS

Cryptocurrencies are more than just digital money. They're a movement toward greater financial inclusion, transparency, and innovation. By reading this book, you're not just learning about a technology; you're stepping into a world of possibilities.

Let's begin your journey into the future of money. Welcome to *Crypto Basics*!

PART ONE

UNDERSTANDING CRYPTOCURRENCIES

CHAPTER ONE: WHAT IS CRYPTOCURRENCY?

Defining cryptocurrency

Cryptocurrency is a form of digital or virtual currency that uses cryptography to secure transactions. Unlike traditional money issued by governments (fiat currency), cryptocurrencies operate on decentralized networks, free from central authority or control.

At its core, cryptocurrency is both a technological and financial innovation. It enables people to transfer value directly to one another, no matter where they are in the world, without relying on banks or intermediaries.

The History of Money and Digital Assets

To understand cryptocurrency, it's helpful to trace the evolution of money:

1. **Bartering**: Trading goods and services directly.

2. **Commodity Money**: Using physical items like gold, silver, or shells as currency.
3. **Fiat Currency**: Government-issued money with no intrinsic value but accepted as a medium of exchange.
4. **Digital Money**: Online banking, credit cards, and mobile payments revolutionized how we interact with money.
5. **Cryptocurrency**: A decentralized digital currency powered by blockchain technology.

Bitcoin, launched in 2009 by an anonymous person or group called Satoshi Nakamoto, was the first cryptocurrency. It introduced the concept of a peer-to-peer digital payment system and laid the foundation for thousands of other cryptocurrencies.

Key Features of Cryptocurrency

- **Decentralization**: No single entity controls the network.

- **Security**: Transactions are secured through cryptography.
- **Transparency**: Blockchain technology ensures that all transactions are publicly verifiable.
- **Global Accessibility**: Anyone with an internet connection can participate.

CHAPTER TWO: BLOCKCHAIN TECHNOLOGY 101

What is Blockchain?

Blockchain is the backbone of cryptocurrency. It's a digital ledger that records transactions across a distributed network of computers. This ensures data integrity, transparency, and security.

Imagine a chain of blocks, where each block contains a list of transactions. Once a block is completed, it links to the next block, forming a chain. This structure makes it nearly impossible to alter past transactions.

How Blockchain Works

1. **Transaction Creation**: A user initiates a transaction.
2. **Verification**: Network participants, called nodes, verify the transaction.
3. **Block Formation**: Verified transactions are grouped into a block.
4. **Consensus Mechanism**: The network agrees on the validity of the

block using mechanisms like Proof of Work (PoW) or Proof of Stake (PoS).
5. **Adding to the Chain**: The block is added to the blockchain, and the transaction becomes permanent.

Types of Blockchain Networks

- **Public**: Open to anyone (e.g., Bitcoin, Ethereum).
- **Private**: Restricted to specific participants (e.g., enterprise blockchains).
- **Hybrid**: Combines elements of public and private blockchains.

Smart Contracts

Smart contracts are self-executing agreements coded into the blockchain. They automatically enforce terms when certain conditions are met. For example, a smart contract could release payment once a product is delivered.

CHAPTER THREE: KEY CRYPTOCURRENCIES

Bitcoin: The Pioneer

Bitcoin (BTC) was the first cryptocurrency and remains the most valuable and widely recognized. It was created to serve as a decentralized alternative to traditional money. Bitcoin is often referred to as "digital gold" due to its finite supply of 21 million coins.

Ethereum: Smart Contract Innovation

Ethereum (ETH) introduced the concept of smart contracts, allowing developers to build decentralized applications (dApps) on its blockchain. This has made Ethereum the foundation of many new crypto projects, from DeFi platforms to NFTs.

Other Notables

- **Binance Coin (BNB)**: Powers the Binance ecosystem.
- **Cardano (ADA)**: Focused on scalability and sustainability.

- **Solana (SOL)**: Known for high-speed and low-cost transactions.

Emerging Cryptos and Trends

New cryptocurrencies regularly enter the market, each promising unique features. Keep an eye on emerging trends like gaming tokens, decentralized identity projects, and environmentally focused cryptocurrencies.

CHAPTER FOUR: THE PURPOSE OF CRYPTOCURRENCIES

Payment Systems
Cryptocurrencies provide an alternative to traditional payment methods, offering lower fees and faster transactions. Bitcoin, Litecoin, and stablecoins like USDT are commonly used for payments.

Investment and Store of Value
Bitcoin, often called "digital gold," is increasingly seen as a hedge against inflation. Many investors hold cryptocurrencies as part of a diversified portfolio.

Decentralized Finance (DeFi)
DeFi platforms offer financial services—like lending, borrowing, and trading—without intermediaries. Examples include Aave, Uniswap, and Compound.

Non-Fungible Tokens (NFTs)
NFTs represent ownership of unique digital assets like art, music, and virtual real estate.

They have opened new avenues for creators and collectors.

PART ONE: WRAP-UP

You now have a foundational understanding of cryptocurrencies: what they are, how they work, and why they matter. In the next part, we'll explore how to get started with crypto—setting up wallets, buying your first coins, and keeping them secure.

PART TWO

GETTING STARTED WITH CRYPTO

CHAPTER FIVE: HOW TO BUY CRYPTOCURRENCY

Setting Up a Wallet

Before purchasing cryptocurrency, you need a wallet to store it. Crypto wallets come in two primary types:

- **Hot Wallets**: Connected to the internet, ideal for frequent transactions (e.g., mobile apps like MetaMask or Trust Wallet).
- **Cold Wallets**: Offline storage for enhanced security (e.g., hardware wallets like Ledger or Trezor).

Steps to set up a wallet:

1. Choose a wallet that suits your needs (hot or cold).
2. Install the wallet software or set up the device.
3. Create a secure backup of your wallet's seed phrase. This phrase is essential for recovering your funds.

Choosing the Right Exchange

Cryptocurrency exchanges are platforms where you can buy, sell, and trade cryptocurrencies. Popular options include:

- **Centralized Exchanges (CEXs)**: User-friendly platforms like Coinbase, Binance, and Kraken.
- **Decentralized Exchanges (DEXs)**: Peer-to-peer platforms like Uniswap and PancakeSwap.

Factors to consider when choosing an exchange:
- Reputation and security history.
- Supported cryptocurrencies.
- Transaction fees.
- Ease of use and customer support.

Navigating Transactions

Once your wallet is set up and you've chosen an exchange, follow these steps:

1. **Sign Up**: Create an account and complete identity verification (if required).

2. **Fund Your Account**: Deposit fiat currency or crypto.
3. **Place an Order**: Choose a cryptocurrency and specify the amount to buy.
4. **Transfer to Your Wallet**: For added security, move your purchased crypto to your wallet.

CHAPTER SIX: STORING CRYPTOCURRENCY SAFELY

Types of Wallets

1. **Hot Wallets**: Ideal for active traders or small amounts. Examples include exchange wallets and mobile apps.
2. **Cold Wallets**: Recommended for long-term storage. Examples include hardware wallets and paper wallets.

Best Practices for Security

- **Use Two-Factor Authentication (2FA)**: Adds an extra layer of protection.
- **Enable Multi-Signature Authorization**: This requires multiple approvals for transactions.
- **Beware of Phishing Scams**: Always double-check links and email senders.

Understanding Private and Public Keys

- **Public Key**: Like your email address, it's shared to receive funds.
- **Private Key**: Like your password, it must never be shared. It's used to access and authorize transactions.

A lost private key often means lost funds, so keep it secure!

CHAPTER SEVEN: INVESTING IN CRYPTOCURRENCY

Risk vs. Reward: What You Need to Know

Cryptocurrencies are highly volatile. Prices can skyrocket or plummet in hours. Always invest only what you can afford to lose.

Popular Investment Strategies

1. **HODLing**: Buying and holding cryptocurrency for the long term.
2. **Trading**: Taking advantage of short-term price movements through day trading or swing trading.
3. **Staking**: Earning rewards by holding and supporting a blockchain network, typically on Proof of Stake (PoS) platforms like Ethereum 2.0 or Cardano.
4. **Dollar-Cost Averaging (DCA)**: Regularly investing a fixed amount regardless of market conditions.

Understanding Market Volatility

- Cryptocurrency prices are influenced by factors like market sentiment, regulations, and technological developments.
- Use tools like price charts and technical indicators to make informed decisions.

PART TWO: WRAP-UP

You're now equipped with the basics of buying, storing, and investing in cryptocurrency. With this knowledge, you can confidently begin your journey into the crypto world. In the next part, we'll explore how crypto is impacting daily life and what the future holds.

PART THREE
CRYPTO IN EVERYDAY LIFE

CHAPTER EIGHT: REAL-WORLD APPLICATIONS

Making Payments

Cryptocurrencies are revolutionizing payments by offering fast, low-cost, and borderless transactions. Popular use cases include:

- **Online Purchases**: Platforms like Overstock and Shopify accept Bitcoin and other cryptos.
- **Cross-Border Payments**: Remittances using crypto bypass traditional banking fees and delays.
- **Micropayments**: Crypto enables tiny transactions that are impractical with traditional methods.

Earning with Crypto

Cryptocurrencies provide new opportunities to generate income.

1. **Mining**: Solving complex problems to validate transactions and earn rewards (e.g., Bitcoin mining).

2. **Staking**: Locking your crypto in a network to earn rewards while supporting its operations.
3. **Yield Farming**: Providing liquidity on DeFi platforms to earn interest or tokens.

Exploring the Metaverse

Cryptocurrency powers virtual worlds where users can interact, trade assets, and build communities.

- **Gaming**: Platforms like Axie Infinity reward players with tokens.
- **Virtual Real Estate**: Users buy, sell, and develop land in metaverses like Decentraland.
- **Digital Economies**: Crypto fuels these ecosystems, from digital wearables to NFT-based assets.

CHAPTER NINE: REGULATIONS AND LEGAL ASPECTS

Understanding the Global Legal Landscape

The regulatory approach to cryptocurrencies varies across the globe.

- **Crypto-Friendly Nations**: Countries like El Salvador, Switzerland, and Singapore have embraced crypto.
- **Restrictive Environments**: Some nations, like China, have banned or heavily regulated crypto activities.

Before engaging in crypto, understand the laws in your jurisdiction to avoid legal pitfalls.

Tax Implications and Reporting

Cryptocurrency transactions often come with tax obligations.

- **Capital Gains Tax**: Applies when selling or trading crypto for a profit.
- **Income Tax**: Staking, mining, or earning crypto as payment may be taxable.

Keep records of all transactions and consult a tax professional familiar with crypto.

Avoiding Scams and Fraud
The crypto space is ripe with opportunities but also risks. Protect yourself by:

- **Verifying Projects**: Research any crypto project before investing.
- **Avoiding "Too Good to Be True" Schemes**: Steer clear of promises of guaranteed high returns.
- **Using Reputable Platforms**: Only transact on trusted wallets and exchanges.

CHAPTER TEN: THE FUTURE OF CRYPTOCURRENCY

Emerging Technologies and Innovations

The crypto space is constantly evolving, with new technologies shaping its future:

- **Layer 2 Solutions**: Enhance blockchain scalability and reduce costs (e.g., Lightning Network).
- **Decentralized Identity**: Systems that allow users to control their digital identity using blockchain.
- **Green Crypto Initiatives**: Projects focused on reducing the environmental impact of crypto.

Mass Adoption Challenges

Cryptocurrency adoption faces barriers, including:

- **Regulatory Uncertainty**: Governments worldwide are still defining crypto regulations.

- **User Experience**: Complex interfaces deter non-technical users.
- **Scalability Issues**: Some blockchains struggle with high transaction volumes.

The Role of Governments and Institutions

While crypto began as a grassroots movement, institutions and governments are increasingly involved.

- **Central Bank Digital Currencies (CBDCs)**: Government-backed digital currencies aim to combine the benefits of crypto with central bank oversight.
- **Institutional Adoption**: Companies like Tesla and MicroStrategy hold Bitcoin as part of their corporate strategy.

PART THREE WRAP-UP

Cryptocurrency is reshaping industries, powering innovation, and influencing how we interact with money, technology, and each other. From practical applications like payments to emerging concepts like the metaverse, the possibilities are limitless.

By understanding crypto's real-world use cases, regulatory environment, and future potential, you're better prepared to navigate and thrive in this dynamic space.

CONCLUSION

Congratulations! You've completed your journey through the basics of cryptocurrency. Whether you're here to invest, use crypto in daily life, or simply understand this transformative technology, you now have the tools and knowledge to participate confidently. The world of cryptocurrency is vast, and your adventure is just beginning.

Stay curious, stay informed, and welcome to the future of money!

APPENDICES

Appendix A: Glossary of Key Terms

1. **Altcoin**: Any cryptocurrency other than Bitcoin. Examples include Ethereum, Litecoin, and Solana.
2. **Blockchain**: A decentralized digital ledger that records transactions across a network of computers.
3. **Cold Wallet**: A cryptocurrency wallet not connected to the internet, offering enhanced security.
4. **Decentralized Finance (DeFi)**: Financial systems built on blockchain networks that operate without intermediaries.
5. **Exchange**: A platform where users can buy, sell, and trade cryptocurrencies.
6. **HODL**: A slang term in the crypto community meaning to hold onto cryptocurrency instead of selling it, regardless of market fluctuations.

7. **Mining**: The process of validating transactions on a blockchain and earning cryptocurrency as a reward.
8. **NFT (Non-Fungible Token)**: A unique digital asset representing ownership of an item such as art, music, or virtual real estate.
9. **Private Key**: A secret code that allows you to access and manage your cryptocurrency.
10. **Smart Contract**: Self-executing code on a blockchain that enforces agreements without intermediaries.

Appendix B: FAQs on Cryptocurrencies

Q1: Is cryptocurrency safe to use?
Cryptocurrency is secure if stored and managed correctly. Use trusted wallets, enable security features like 2FA, and never share your private keys.

Q2: How do I know which cryptocurrency to invest in?
Research projects thoroughly. Look for strong use cases, active development teams, and community engagement. Only invest what you can afford to lose.

Q3: Can I lose all my money in crypto?
Yes, due to market volatility, scams, or loss of private keys. Always exercise caution and follow best practices for security.

Q4: What's the difference between a token and a coin?

- **Coin**: Operates on its own blockchain (e.g., Bitcoin, Ethereum).

- **Token**: Built on an existing blockchain (e.g., Tether on Ethereum).

Q5: Are cryptocurrencies legal?

Legality varies by country. Research your local laws and regulations regarding buying, holding, and trading crypto.

Appendix C: Recommended Tools, Wallets, and Exchanges

Wallets

- **Hot Wallets**: MetaMask, Trust Wallet, Exodus
- **Cold Wallets**: Ledger Nano X, Trezor Model T

Exchanges

- **Centralized**: Binance, Coinbase, Kraken
- **Decentralized**: Uniswap, PancakeSwap, SushiSwap

Portfolio Trackers

- CoinMarketCap, CoinGecko, Blockfolio

CLOSING NOTE

Cryptocurrency is an exciting and rapidly changing field. Stay updated, continue learning, and remember that understanding the basics is just the first step in your journey. With the tools and resources provided, you're now ready to explore the world of crypto confidently.

www.ingramcontent.com/pod-product-compliance
Lightning Source LLC
Chambersburg PA
CBHW070942220526
45469CB00007B/2483